SELECTED POEMS OF
CHRISTINA ROSSETTI

SELECTED POEMS OF
CHRISTINA ROSSETTI
1830 –1894

METHUEN

This selection first published in Great Britain by Methuen 2005
Copyright © 2005 by Methuen Publishing Ltd

Methuen Publishing Ltd
215 Vauxhall Bridge Road
London SW1V 1EJ
www.methuen.co.uk

Methuen Publishing Limited Reg. No. 3543167

ISBN 0 413 77506 2

1 3 5 7 9 10 8 6 4 2

A CIP catalogue for this title
is available from the British Library.

Printed and bound in Great Britain
by St Edmundsbury Press, Bury St Edmunds, Suffolk

Contents

Spring Quiet

GONE were but the Winter,
　Come were but the Spring,
I would go to a covert
　Where the birds sing;

Where in the whitethorn
　Singeth a thrush,
And a robin sings
　In the holly-bush.

Full of fresh scents
　Are the budding boughs
Arching high over
　A cool green house;

Full of sweet scents,
　And whispering air
Which sayeth softly:
　'We spread no snare;

'Here dwell in safety,
    Here dwell alone,
With a clear stream
    And a mossy stone.

'Here the sun shineth
    Most shadily;
Here is heard an echo
    Of the far sea,
        Tho' far off it be.'

In the Willow Shade

I SAT beneath a willow tree,
　　Where water falls and calls;
While fancies upon fancies solaced me,
　　Some true, and some were false.

Who set their heart upon a hope
　　That never comes to pass,
Droop in the end like fading heliotrope
　　The sun's wan looking-glass.

Who set their will upon a whim
　　Clung to through good and ill,
Are wrecked alike whether they sink or swim,
　　Or hit or miss their will.

All things are vain that wax and wane,
　　For which we waste our breath;
Love only doth not wane and is not vain,
　　Love only outlives death.

A singing lark rose toward the sky,
    Circling he sang amain;
He sang, a speck scarce visible sky-high,
    And then he sank again.

A second like a sunlit spark
    Flashed singing up his track;
But never overtook that foremost lark,
    And songless fluttered back.

A hovering melody of birds
    Haunted the air above;
They clearly sang contentment without words,
    And youth and joy and love.

O silvery weeping willow tree
    With all leaves shivering,
Have you no purpose but to shadow me
    Beside this rippled spring?

On this first fleeting day of Spring,
    For Winter is gone by,
And every bird on every quivering wing
    Floats in a sunny sky;

On this first Summer-like soft day,
    While sunshine steeps the air,
And every cloud has gat itself away,
    And birds sing everywhere.

Have you no purpose in the world
    But thus to shadow me
With all your tender drooping twigs unfurled,
    O weeping willow tree?

With all your tremulous leaves outspread
    Betwixt me and the sun,
While here I loiter on a mossy bed
    With half my work undone;

My work undone, that should be done
    At once with all my might;
For after the long day and lingering sun
    Comes the unworking night.

This day is lapsing on its way,
    Is lapsing out of sight;
And after all the chances of the day
    Comes the resourceless night.

The weeping willow shook its head
 And stretched its shadow long;
The west grew crimson, the sun smoldered red,
 The birds forbore a song.

Slow wind sighed through the willow leaves,
 The ripple made a moan,
The world drooped murmuring like a thing that
   grieves;
 And then I felt alone.

I rose to go, and felt the chill,
 And shivered as I went;
Yet shivering wondered, and I wonder still,
 What more that willow meant;

That silvery weeping willow tree
 With all leaves shivering,
Which spent one long day overshadowing me
 Beside a spring in Spring.

In an Artist's Studio

ONE face looks out from all his canvasses,
   One selfsame figure sits or walks or leans;
   We found her hidden just behind those screens,
That mirror gave back all her loveliness.
A queen in opal or in ruby dress,
   A nameless girl in freshest summer greens,
   A saint, an angel; – every canvas means
The same one meaning, neither more nor less.
He feeds upon her face by day and night,
   And she with true kind eyes looks back on
   him,
Fair as the moon and joyful as the light:
   Not wan with waiting, not with sorrow dim;
Not as she is, but was when hope shone bright;
   Not as she is, but as she fills his dream.

'No, Thank You, John'

I NEVER said I loved you, John:
    Why will you teaze me day by day,
And wax a weariness to think upon
    With always 'do' and 'pray'?

You know I never loved you, John;
    No fault of mine made me your toast:
Why will you haunt me with a face as wan
    As shows an hour-old ghost?

I dare say Meg or Moll would take
    Pity upon you, if you'd ask:
And pray don't remain single for my sake
    Who can't perform that task.

I have no heart? – Perhaps I have not;
    But then you're mad to take offence
That I don't give you what I have not got:
    Use your own common sense.

Let bygones be bygones:
    Don't call me false, who owed not to be true:
I'd rather answer 'No' to fifty Johns
    Than answer 'Yes' to you.

Let's mar our pleasant days no more,
    Song-birds of passage, days of youth:
Catch at today, forget the days before:
    I'll wink at your untruth.

Let us strike hands as hearty friends;
    No more, no less; and friendship's good:
Only don't keep in view ulterior ends,
    And points not understood

In open treaty. Rise above
    Quibbles and shuffling off and on:
Here's friendship for you if you like; but love, –
    No, thank you, John.

Song

Oн roses for the flush of youth,
　And laurel for the perfect prime;
But pluck an ivy branch for me
　Grown old before my time.

Oh violets for the grave of youth,
　And bay for those dead in their prime;
Give me the withered leaves I chose
　Before in the old time.

A Birthday

My heart is like a singing bird
   Whose nest is in a watered shoot;
My heart is like an apple tree
   Whose boughs are bent with thickset
   fruit;
My heart is like a rainbow shell
   That paddles in a halcyon sea;
My heart is gladder than all these
   Because my love is come to me.

Raise me a dais of silk and down;
   Hang it with vair and purple dyes;
Carve it in doves and pomegranates,
   And peacocks with a hundred eyes;
Work it in gold and silver grapes,
   In leaves and silver fleurs-de-lys;
Because the birthday of my life
   Is come, my love is come to me.

May

I CANNOT tell you how it was;
But this I know: it came to pass
Upon a bright and breezy day
When May was young; ah pleasant May!
As yet the poppies were not born
Between the blades of tender corn;
The last egg had not hatched as yet,
Nor any bird foregone its mate.

I cannot tell you what it was;
But this I know: it did but pass.
It passed away with sunny May,
With all sweet things it passed away,
And left me old, and cold, and grey.

The Thread of Life

I

The irresponsive silence of the land,
  The irresponsive sounding of the sea,
  Speak both one message of one sense to me:–
Aloof, aloof, we stand aloof, so stand
Thou too aloof bound with the flawless band
  Of inner solitude; we bind not thee;
  But who from thy self-chain shall set thee free?
What heart shall touch thy heart? what hand thy
    hand? –
And I am sometimes proud and sometimes meek,
  And sometimes I remember days of old
When fellowship seemed not so far to seek
  And all the world and I seemed much less cold,
And at the rainbow's foot lay surely gold,
  And hope felt strong and life itself not weak.

II

Thus am I mine own prison. Everything
  Around me free and sunny and at ease:
  Or if in shadow, in a shade of trees
Which the sun kisses, where the gay birds sing
And where all winds make various murmuring;

Where bees are found, with honey for the
bees;
Where sounds are music, and where silences
Are music of an unlike fashioning.
Then gaze I at the merrymaking crew,
    And smile a moment and a moment sigh
Thinking, Why can I not rejoice with you?
    But soon I put the foolish fancy by:
I am not what I have nor what I do;
    But what I was I am, I am even I.

III

Therefore myself is that one only thing
    I hold to use or waste, to keep or give;
    My sole possession every day I live,
And still mine own despite Time's winnowing.
Ever mine own, while moons and seasons bring
    From crudeness ripeness mellow and sanative;
    Ever mine own, till Death shall ply his sieve;
And still mine own, when saints break grave and
    sing.
And this myself as king unto my King
    I give, to Him Who gave Himself for me;
Who gives Himself to me, and bids me sing
    A sweet new song of His redeemed set free;
He bids me sing: O death, where is thy sting?
    And sing: O grave, where is thy victory?

Remember

REMEMBER me when I am gone away,
   Gone far away into the silent land;
   When you can no more hold me by the
   hand,
Nor I half turn to go yet turning stay.
Remember me when no more day by day
   You tell me of our future that you planned:
   Only remember me; you understand
It will be late to counsel then or pray.
Yet if you should forget me for a while
   And afterwards remember, do not grieve:
   For if the darkness and corruption leave
   A vestige of the thoughts that once I had,
Better by far you should forget and smile
   Than that you should remember and be sad.

An Apple-Gathering

I PLUCKED pink blossoms from mine apple tree
   And wore them all that evening in my hair:
Then in due season when I went to see
    I found no apples there.

With dangling basket all along the grass
   As I had come I went the selfsame track:
My neighbours mocked me while they saw me pass
    So empty-handed back.

Lilian and Lilias smiled in trudging by,
   Their heaped-up basket teazed me like a jeer;
Sweet-voiced they sang beneath the sunset sky,
    Their mother's home was near.

Plump Gertrude passed me with her basket full,
   A stronger hand than hers helped it along;
A voice talked with her thro' the shadows cool
    More sweet to me than song.

Ah Willie, Willie, was my love less worth
   Than apples with their green leaves piled above?
I counted rosiest apples on the earth
    Of far less worth than love.

So once it was with me you stooped to talk
   Laughing and listening in this very lane:
To think that by this way we used to walk
    We shall not walk again!

I let my neighbours pass me, ones and twos
   And groups; the latest said the night grew chill,
And hastened: but I loitered, while the dews
    Fell fast I loitered still.

Grown And Flown

I LOVED my love from green of Spring
   Until sere Autumn's fall;
But now that leaves are withering
   How should one love at all?
   One heart's too small
For hunger, cold, love, everything.

I loved my love on sunny days
   Until late Summer's wane;
But now that frost begins to glaze
   How should one love again?
   Nay, love and pain
Walk wide apart in diverse ways.

I loved my love – alas to see
   That this should be, alas!
I thought that this could scarcely be,
   Yet has it come to pass:
   Sweet sweet love was,
Now bitter bitter grown to me.

from
Sing-Song

Baby lies so fast asleep
  That we cannot wake her:
Will the Angels clad in white
  Fly from heaven to take her?

Baby lies so fast asleep
  That no pain can grieve her;
Put a snowdrop in her hand,
  Kiss her once and leave her.

Song: 'When I am dead'

When I am dead, my dearest,
　Sing no sad songs for me;
Plant thou no roses at my head,
　Nor shady cypress tree:
Be the green grass above me
　With showers and dewdrops wet;
And if thou wilt, remember,
　And if thou wilt, forget.

I shall not see the shadows,
　I shall not feel the rain;
I shall not hear the nightingale
　Sing on, as if in pain:
And dreaming through the twilight
　That doth not rise nor set,
Haply I may remember,
　And haply may forget.

Summer is Ended

To think that this meaningless thing was ever a
  rose,
    Scentless, colourless, *this*!
  Will it ever be thus (who knows?)
      Thus with our bliss,
  If we wait till the close?

Tho' we care not to wait for the end, there comes
  the end
    Sooner, later, at last,
  Which nothing can mar, nothing mend:
      An end locked fast,
  Bent we cannot re-bend.

Dream-Land

WHERE sunless rivers weep
Their waves into the deep,
She sleeps a charmèd sleep:
    Awake her not.
Led by a single star,
She came from very far
To seek where shadows are
    Her pleasant lot.

She left the rosy morn,
She left the fields of corn,
For twilight cold and lorn
    And water springs.
Thro' sleep, as thro' a veil,
She sees the sky look pale,
And hears the nightingale
    That sadly sings.

Rest, rest, a perfect rest
Shed over brow and breast;
Her face is toward the west,
    The purple land.

She cannot see the grain
Ripening on hill and plain;
She cannot feel the rain
    Upon her hand.

Rest, rest, for evermore
Upon a mossy shore;
Rest, rest at the heart's core
    Till time shall cease:
Sleep that no pain shall wake;
Night that no morn shall break,
Till joy shall overtake
    Her perfect peace.

A Daughter of Eve

A FOOL I was to sleep at noon,
   And wake when night is chilly
Beneath the comfortless cold moon;
A fool to pluck my rose too soon,
   A fool to snap my lily.

My garden-plot I have not kept;
   Faded and all-forsaken,
I weep as I have never wept:
Oh it was summer when I slept,
   It's winter now I waken.

Talk what you please of future Spring
   And sun-warmed sweet tomorrow: –
Stripped bare of hope and everything,
No more to laugh, no more to sing,
   I sit alone with sorrow.

Bitter for Sweet

SUMMER is gone with all its roses,
   Its sun and perfumes and sweet flowers,
   Its warm air and refreshing showers:
      And even Autumn closes.

Yea, Autumn's chilly self is going,
   And winter comes which is yet colder;
   Each day the hoar-frost waxes bolder,
      And the last buds cease blowing.

Winter: My Secret

I TELL my secret? No indeed, not I!
Perhaps some day, who knows?
But not today; it froze, and blows, and snows,
And you're too curious: fie!
You want to hear it? well:
Only, my secret's mine, and I won't tell.

Or, after all, perhaps there's none:
Suppose there is no secret after all,
But only just my fun.
Today's a nipping day, a biting day;
In which one wants a shawl,
A veil, a cloak, and other wraps:
I cannot ope to every one who taps,
And let the draughts come whistling thro' my hall;
Come bounding and surrounding me,
Come buffeting, astounding me,
Nipping and clipping thro' my wraps and all.
I wear my mask for warmth: who ever shows
His nose to Russian snows
To be pecked at by every wind that blows?
You would not peck? I thank you for good will,
Believe, but leave that truth untested still.

Spring's an expansive time: yet I don't trust
March with its peck of dust,
Nor April with its rainbow-crowned brief showers,
Nor even May, whose flowers
One frost may wither thro' the sunless hours.

Perhaps some languid summer day,
When drowsy birds sing less and less,
And golden fruit is ripening to excess,
If there's not too much sun nor too much cloud,
And the warm wind is neither still nor loud,
Perhaps my secret I may say,
Or you may guess.

Up-hill

Does the road wind up-hill all the way?
    Yes, to the very end.
Will the day's journey take the whole long day?
    From morn to night, my friend.

But is there for the night a resting-place?
    A roof for when the slow dark hours begin.
May not the darkness hide it from my face?
    You cannot miss that inn.

Shall I meet other wayfarers at night?
    Those who have gone before.
Then must I knock, or call when just in sight?
    They will not keep you standing at that door.

Shall I find comfort, travel-sore and weak?
    Of labour you shall find the sum.
Will there be beds for me and all who seek?
    Yea, beds for all who come.

A Christmas Carol

In the bleak mid-winter
  Frosty wind made moan,
Earth stood hard as iron,
  Water like a stone;
Snow had fallen, snow on snow,
  Snow on snow,
In the bleak mid-winter
  Long ago.

Our God, Heaven cannot hold Him
  Nor earth sustain;
Heaven and earth shall flee away
  When He comes to reign:
In the bleak mid-winter
  A stable-place sufficed
The Lord God Almighty
  Jesus Christ.

Enough for Him, whom cherubim
  Worship night and day,
A breastful of milk
  And a mangerful of hay;
Enough for Him whom angels
  Fall down before,

The ox and ass and camel
  Which adore.

Angels and archangels
  May have gathered there,
Cherubim and seraphim
  Throng'd the air:
But only His mother
  In her maiden bliss
Worshipped the Beloved
  With a kiss.

What can I give Him,
  Poor as I am?
If I were a shepherd
  I would bring a lamb,
If I were a wise man
  I would do my part, –
Yet what I can I give Him,
  Give my heart.

'Passing away,
saith the World'

PASSING away, saith the World, passing away:
Chances, beauty and youth sapped day by day:
Thy life never continueth in one stay.
Is the eye waxen dim, is the dark hair changing to grey
That hath won neither laurel nor bay?
I shall clothe myself in Spring and bud in May:
Thou, root-stricken, shalt not rebuild thy decay
On my bosom for aye.
Then I answered: Yea.

Passing away, saith my Soul, passing away:
With its burden of fear and hope, of labour and play;
Hearken what the past doth witness and say:
Rust in thy gold, a moth is in thine array,
A canker is in thy bud, thy leaf must decay.
At midnight, at cockcrow, at morning, one certain day
Lo the bridegroom shall come and shall not delay:
Watch thou and pray.
Then I answered: Yea.

Passing away, saith my God, passing away:
Winter passeth after the long delay:

New grapes on the vine, new figs on the tender spray,
Turtle calleth turtle in Heaven's May.
Tho' I tarry, wait for Me, trust Me, watch and pray.
Arise, come away, night is past and lo it is day,
My love, My sister, My spouse, thou shalt hear Me say.
Then I answered: Yea.

Winter Rain

Every valley drinks,
  Every dell and hollow:
Where the kind rain sinks and sinks,
  Green of Spring will follow.

Yet a lapse of weeks
  Buds will burst their edges,
Strip their wool-coats, glue-coats, streaks,
  In the woods and hedges;

Weave a bower of love
  For birds to meet each other,
Weave a canopy above
  Nest and egg and mother.

But for fattening rain
  We should have no flowers,
Never a bud or leaf again
  But for soaking showers;

Never a mated bird
   In the rocking tree-tops,
Never indeed a flock or herd
   To graze upon the lea-crops.

Lambs so woolly white,
   Sheep the sun-bright leas on,
They could have no grass to bite
   But for rain in season.

We should find no moss
   In the shadiest places,
Find no waving meadow grass
   Pied with broad-eyed daisies:

But miles of barren sand,
   With never a son or daughter,
Not a lily on the land,
   Or lily on the water.

Twilight Calm

OH, pleasant eventide!
  Clouds on the western side
Grow grey and greyer, hiding the warm sun:
The bees and birds, their happy labours done,
  Seek their close nests and bide.

  Screened in the leafy wood
  The stock-doves sit and brood:
The very squirrel leaps from bough to bough
But lazily; pauses; and settles now
  Where once he stored his food.

  One by one the flowers close,
  Lily and dewy rose
Shutting their tender petals from the moon:
The grasshoppers are still; but not so soon
  Are still the noisy crows.

  The dormouse squats and eats
  Choice little dainty bits
Beneath the spreading roots of a broad lime
Nibbling his fill he stops from time to time
  And listens where he sits.

From far the lowings come
Of cattle driven home:
From farther still the wind brings fitfully
The vast continual murmur of the sea,
   Now loud, now almost dumb.

The gnats whirl in the air,
The evening gnats; and there
The owl opes broad his eyes and wings to sail
For prey; the bat wakes; and the shell-less snail
   Comes forth, clammy and bare.

Hark! that's the nightingale,
Telling the selfsame tale
Her song told when this ancient earth was young:
So echoes answered when her song was sung
   In the first wooded vale.

We call it love and pain
The passion of her strain;
And yet we little understand or know:
Why should it not be rather joy that so
   Throbs in each throbbing vein?

In separate herds the deer
Lie; here the bucks, and here
The does, and by its mother sleeps the fawn:
Through all the hours of night until the dawn
They sleep, forgetting fear.

The hare sleeps where it lies,
With wary half-closed eyes;
The cock has ceased to crow, the hen to cluck:
Only the fox is out, some heedless duck
Or chicken to surprise.

Remote, each single star
Comes out, till there they are
All shining brightly: how the dews fall damp!
While close at hand the glow-worm lights her lamp,
Or twinkles from afar.

But evening now is done
As much as if the sun
Day-giving had arisen in the East:
For night has come; and the great calm has ceased,
The quiet sands have run.

Rest

O EARTH, lie heavily upon her eyes;
Seal her sweet eyes weary of watching, Earth;
　　Lie close around her; leave no room for mirth
With its harsh laughter, nor for sound of sighs.
She hath no questions, she hath no replies,
　　Hushed in and curtained with a blessed
　　dearth
　　Of all that irked her from the hour of birth;
With stillness that is almost Paradise.
Darkness more clear than noonday holdeth her,
　　Silence more musical than any song;
Even her very heart has ceased to stir:
Until the morning of Eternity
Her rest shall not begin nor end, but be;
　　And when she wakes she will not think it
　　long.

Another Spring

IF I might see another Spring
   I'd not plant summer flowers and wait:
I'd have my crocuses at once,
My leafless pink mezereons,
   My chill-veined snowdrops, choicer yet
   My white or azure violet,
Leaf-nested primrose; anything
      To blow at once, not late.

If I might see another Spring
   I'd listen to the daylight birds
That build their nests and pair and sing,
Nor wait for mateless nightingale;
   I'd listen to the lusty herds,
   The ewes with lambs as white as snow,
I'd find out music in the hail
      And all the winds that blow.

If I might see another Spring –
    Oh stinging comment on my past
That all my past results in 'if' –
If I might see another Spring
    I'd laugh today, today is brief
    I would not wait for anything:
I'd use today that cannot last,
      Be glad today and sing.